WAY OF THE FEATHER

Indigenoius Protocols

One Who Catches Lightning and Keeper of the Thunderstone

BIG LITTLE LIFE PUBLISHING LLC

Contents

To the bird kingdom.

Those alive and those who have become extinct due to human lack of imagination to live a life of balance and reci-procity.

To the pigeon who shows us the resilience and adaptability to continue to live despite being undervalued by a colonial society which develops through the devaluation of beings and resources.

And to my human teachers both Indigenous and non indigenous who inspire me to keep connecting and the dedicated few helpers that brought this book to life.

ONE WHO CATCHES LIGHTNING AND KEEPER OF THE THUNDERSTONE

ABOUT THE AUTHOR

An indigenous wisdom keeper and elder. Their lineage is Zapotec, Purapecha and Sephardine and have extensive spiritual training with Lakota, Mayan, Aztec, Apache, Hawaiian and Hopi traditions.

Chosen at birth and trained since then to be a bridge walker, carrying the wisdom of multiple indigenous lineages, and weaving them together with an understanding of modern, rapidly changing contexts, to support a grounded, radical path of healing for individuals and the collective.

A formally trained fine artist and filmmaker, a singer-songwriter who has released multiple albums, a published poet, a motivational speaker, metaphysical healer with training in multiple modalities, a guide and mentor to people of all ages and backgrounds, a teacher with years of unique original curriculum, and of course always a student, learner and seeker.

INTRO

"Once we start to act, hope is everywhere." - Greta Thunberg

"In my people's language we do not have a word for hope, we have instead prayer and action, this is why we come to sweatlodge." - Walking Eagle Karuk Elder

While one might see the similarities in these statements, the cultural and contextual differences set the stage for this cultural exchange. Words, even in a common language, have very different meanings. The questions that one must always have are how does one "consume" culture? How were you raised to appreciate, appropriate, dismiss, dismantle, or eradicate something that is different from you? Why must we keep this in mind? Because this will be the lens that everything passes through, so we must recognize the cognitive biases one might have. Why? Only until you know, will you be able to grow, and growth is at the center of Indigenous ways. Not just the privileged personal narcissistic growth of the Western individual, but that of all beings on this planet, in relation to all.

Prayer and action.

1. We must recognize we have power -if you feel powerless, then own that feeling and instead of giving up on it, have courage and compas-

sion. If we start here, admitting where we are and what gift we have to give, that is enough. When I say gift, I mean the gift of honesty; the honesty of your powerlessness and the feeling itself. How can powerlessness be a gift? Because it is you at a certain time and place. And you are a gift.

Others would say the feeling is not you so do not grasp it. But we can not deny the energy of emotions and their embodiment. So accept them. Accept yourself. Instead of judging yourself for feeling powerless, I urge you to be curious. Curious where this feeling comes from, where it sits in your body, and how long it remains. In other words, be curious about the power you have to create emotion. Ahh there it is, you are powerful even in your powerlessness.

Your mind isn't your enemy, the idea of your mind is.

People think of intelligence as being of the mind not nature.

Your mind is powerful, use its power to create the beauty you desire. We demonize the mind so many times because we can't control it. We think control is next to godliness. It is this type of thinking that takes us away from the natural blueprint of who we are; creatures with creative minds. When we take away the instinctive nature of our being, we do not embody the truth of who we are and the wildness of our duality. We take nature out of nurture, and in doing so cut off the connection with Mother Earth and her creativity.

"Just understand your mind; how it works, how attachment and desire arise, how ignorance arises, and where emotions come from. It is sufficient to know the nature of all that; that alone can bring you happiness and peace. Thus, your life can change completely; everything turns upside down. What you once interpreted as horrible can become beautiful."

— Lama Thubten Yeshe, 1975, *Make Your Mind an Ocean,* Lama Yeshe Wisdom Archive.

The mind is part of us, and we are part of nature. Your thoughts run like a river. There are mountains inside of you. When we look at the mind as part of nature and not separate from it, we can commune more deeply with Mother Earth. We can hear what she is asking of us.

Meditate in that way.

Notice how the river of your thoughts runs.

Is it fast, slow, deep?

Colonization keeps separating the mind from the body, from nature, from our instincts and intuition. Even mindfulness points to the mind being separate. AI takes this even further in the sense that its intelligence is based on mined data which it has run out of. To "think" is to be connected, not to interpret or regurgitate, but to be in the vulnerability of just one of many.

If we can start imagining the nature of our mind as one with the Earth that will help us build the bridge. Earth intelligence is what we need more of right now. We need you. Not some version manipulated by a learning machine that creates artifice.

2. We must recognize the power of our actions and the ramifications of how they affect others. In the case of the quote above, Greta is talking about climate change. The deeper question she raises is that of culture change, so the question is raised again: what will you change? We need to recognize that non-action is still action, and the consequences of that inaction. In other words all our hands are stained.

"Meditation does not matter that much if it has no effect on the rest of our life. Likewise, we could be filled with empty words that do not lead to any change whatsoever in our life or our relationship with others. We need to act on our understanding and our awareness."

—Judy Lief, 2016 *Meditation alone is not enough*, Tricycle

Only once we recognize this truth and not judge it, can we then see the potential violence of non- action equal to the potential peace that action can create. Here once again we can recognize our power, the power to choose, which then in turn creates not just our reality but contributes to the collective. In other words, we can not stop change nor deny change that occurs based on whatever "we do" or "not do", because both contain the power to create emotion - energy in motion.

"In trying to deny that things are always changing, we lose our sense of the sacredness of life. It's easy to forget that life and death are part of the natural scheme of things, intrinsic to our lives in an eternally shifting universe."

—Ronna Kabatznick, 2014, *Sea of Sorrow,* Tricycle

So then the question arises again:

What action, big or small, will you take today to change your life?

The power is yours to choose. The question is: are your actions, or non-actions, creating the world and reality that you want? Continuing to do the same thing and expecting a different result? That is not attainable and we all know that is just madness. So if you want to stop the madness, what will you choose to change? How will you choose to change your life ? How will you change the world? Most importantly, who will you be at every moment of this process which we call life?

By accepting the power and responsibility to change ourselves, and getting the help and support we need to do so, no one walks alone. The myth of the lone wolf is not true, (trust me I walk with wolves) the wolf is just looking for its place in the collective.

We are in a critical time in the history of humankind. Which *way* will you decide to go? The fork in the road is threefold. What will you choose?

Continuing to hand over your sovereignty to AI, governments and corporations, to give up your spiritual path and return to slumber? Or to remember the old ways of deep relationship, where all beings are free.

Are you ready to begin the work of being? Where healing isn't about something that is wrong with you, but where you are fascinated, where you have fallen in love with the notion of being completely you. *You are enough*. Whether you have that spark at the beginning or you find it through the process of re-discovering yourself, may you have the courage to know that any step is good enough, as long as you are doing so in a reciprocal way with yourself, with other people, and with mother nature.

Create your life within community.

This is the way of the Indigenous and to create it one can not just imitate it in dress or songs. There are deep rooted connections that come to us as protocols. These are not limitations but the rich mud where we plant the roots of relation. These protocols, while different from nation to nation, there is one way of relating that ties us all together: We are. In being. So we recognize we are no greater or lesser than any being, a sign of the true humility we walk with. This means there is no "separation", no one beings greatness is individual, as the West has defined. The self as modernity has created is not the Indigenous one. We are. I am. Individuating within the whole and never apart. Interdependence is the path

Wisdom keeping

The teachings shared here in this format as well as in other formats at The Path of IX are a compilation of over 47 years of training, study and earning. Chosen at birth for this path and earning the names One Who Catches Lightning and Keeper of the Thunderstone, the keeping of this wisdom comes through the birth lineages of Zapotec, Purapecha, Otomi and Sephardine and extensive training includes work in the Lakota, Mayan, Aztec, Hopi and Hawaiian traditions.

How to use this book

There are 2 parts:

1. The Protocols: Following the seasonality and intelligence of the sacred hoop, these protocols are grounded in the biospheres of each direction.

2. Feathers: How to gather, their meanings and the process of each one's lesson, feathering a nest and working with the slow medicine of creating with our hands.

This book is a companion to the self paced class "The Way of The Feather" and can be used as part of it or as a whole in itself.

This book, as well as all of the offerings at the Path of IX are part of our Slow Medicine offerings to increase your Earth Intelligence. Take your time and come back to this guide at different times of the day, month, and years.

We have done our best to simply state complex teachings that are thousands of years old but beware of their simplicity, to not think of them as "simple" or "easy" or that the act of reading alone will open these protocols to you. These teachings are vastly complex and take time to grow from seed to sapling to large tree as you tend to your relations. This isn't poetry but a call to plant a tree and grow with it. We hope you approach these teachings with the grace, mercy, universal love and compassion they were written in and passed down.

Part I

Way Of the Feather

The way of the feather is one of yearning, learning, earning and letting go.

Indigenous ways are regenerative. Indigenous ways are not about hoarding but about being a part of a complete cycle of birth and death. They are not limited to the lifetime of one person or being; there is a belief of a collective consciousness and connection, which expands beyond time and space as defined by humans. Our ancestors knew this. They did not chart the skies, rivers, and land to conquer them but to observe them and become part of the song of creation.

To live well is to add to this consciousness, including our fears, failures, losses, as well as triumphs and how we work with our desires and motivations. To be a good relation is to stay connected at all times - to not isolate or disassociate- no matter what the conditions. It is not easy to be a good relation, to oneself, to Earth, to all beings, to creation and destruction itself.

Yet, this is the way of the feather, one in which the goal is to reach the true enlightenment of knowing nothing. To let go of all conditions, all achievements. To accept what you do not know is far greater and will always remain larger than your life and to rest in this and know you are, and that simply being is enough. Even the Bible teaches in

Matthew 6:26 "look at the birds of the air; they neither sow or reap or gather into barns". Birds teach us many things, one of them being to not accumulate or spend time worrying about becoming an expert.

To acclimate ourselves to this new way of being, we will follow the map of the circle, or as it is known as the sacred directions. For the purposes of this guide we must remember that there is not one universal circle or right way to speak of the directions. Why? Our ancestors all came from different places and ways of navigation, so the elements might be different because they are based on the ecology, typography or, what I like to call, the biosphere of where they lived at the time.

Circles are a type of social technology

When the West speaks of Indigenous peoples and societies, most of the reference point is half clothed people running in the Amazon, or the American West where "Indians lived in t-pees". With that there is an underlying bias that Indigenous things are simple, easy to learn, conquer, and use.

Whether romanced or not, there is a level of forgetting the vast empires of the Maya, Inca, Purapecha, Otomi, Aztec, and many more, with complex systems of communication, universities, art, cosmology, armies, agriculture and the list goes on.

Indigenous peoples have many "circles", protocols, and each one is vastly different and unique to places as well as people. There is no "one way" or "saviorship" when it comes to our ways. Instead we have vast and deep knowledge systems of interrelated connection, which is not human centric at its core.

Defining human-centric a simplified definition

To not be human-centric does not mean you do not like humans. Instead it means you do not subscribe to the colonized notion that humans are superior to other beings on this planet. Therefore, you do not subscribe to human beings as the ones who create value and worth; for example, a human-centric society believes a building has more value than a natural tree. It places value on humans creating things from extraction and sees Earth as a resource. There was a time and there still exists, this way of being, not just as a philosophy but as a lived and breathed experience. It is not limited to jungles or countryside, many present day nations live like this. The issue is that when you walk around with a colonial mindset your value point has been created in a human-centric way, so this is the point that needs to shift, to reveal a possibility beyond. There's no way of critically thinking yourself out of this mindset, but there is a way of slowly walking around the circle and its sacred directions; walking around the circle starts to unravel this programming, a little bit at a time.

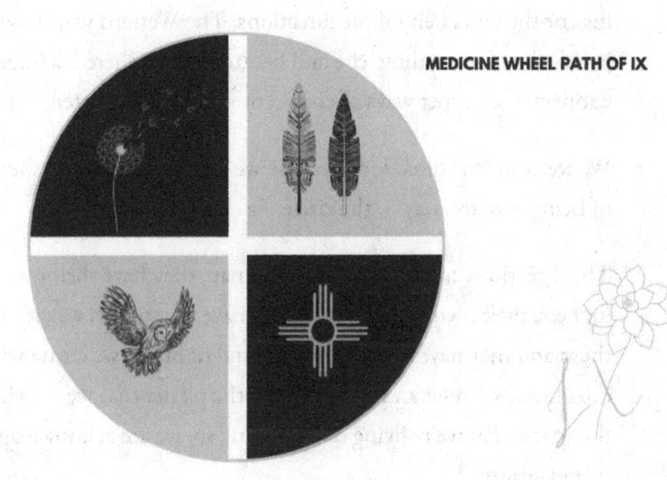
MEDICINE WHEEL PATH OF IX

The Sacred Directions

Many have written about the sacred directions and they share the traditions that they come from and what they mean. Almost all Indigenous cultures have a relationship to the directions which include elements, spirit animals, plant beings, a time in your life and more.

Many learn this checklist way and repeat it. While repeating keeps these connections alive not many have been taught the deeper meanings or the whys behind the directions. The Western world uses them just as they use anything else and because of this there is a huge disconnect, the deeper ways of connection remain forgotten.

We welcome the directions because we are acknowledging these ways of beingness, the way of the circle.

The directions aren't just points in a map, they have their own beingness, their own intelligence. They have that which we create with them and they have in their own natural right. As we create with the directions, we reset and acknowledge the planet that we're living on, the spaces that we're living on. By doing so, we are acknowledging sacred ground.

As we acknowledge sacred ground, we acknowledge relationships, we walk around this circle.

We will use the path of the circle to support this process of , The Way of the Feather, recognizing that birds, whether migratory or not, instinctively follow the natural rhythms of the directions as they are tuned into seasons.

Entering the circle - A practical meditation

If you prefer to listen to the meditation please go to episode 66 of the podcast "Walking with our shadow"

With gratitude, grace and thanksgiving, we address the direction of the East and the guardian spirits of the East, of whatever tradition you come from. Allow yourself this time in the East. The East always reminds us, with that rising sun, we get to begin again. At any point in this practice, or in this book where you feel lost, or need to get back, remember that the East is holding that opportunity for us to begin again. Thank the East.

Now moving down and around to the South. We greet, we welcome and we ask the South and the guardians of the South to hold us in this circle today. The South is that place where things become bone and flesh. This is really the beginning of incarnation, or the physical reality of life. It's where we are created. This is why it's called the place of the student. This is where we get to go back and sit in the South whenever we want, not just to learn, but to create. For some the East is water, the beginning, the idea, the void, enlightenment, and then the south moves us really into the birth, incarnation, our mission on this planet, on this plane, then we move up and around to the West.

As we greet the West, asking the West to hold and to witness us in the circle. Allow yourself to be in each of these points. It's not just about you greeting them, it's about you receiving. You're asking to be held. You're asking to be witnessed, you are entering into a relationship. The relationship of the West is the opportunity to be with thunder beings and lightning and pressure systems and storms and wind; a part of nature that we think we cannot see or does not affect us, but affects everything. It is one of the hottest parts of sweat lodge. It's where in some traditions leaders sit, because then they can face the East, that place of remembering and enlightenment, enlightenment in the sense of staying connected to the memory and to the promise, the road and the path that we're on - in this case the East, to begin again. With that we give gratitude to the West.

We move up to the North. Here we discover where our bones rest, our ancestors, where we return back to the soil. We ask the North to witness us, to hold us, to be in relationship with us, with this medicine that it brings to us - not just connection to our ancestors, but connection to the cycle of life itself.

We come back down to the East, and we acknowledge the direction below us, The Earth, who is our mother, our grandmother, who holds us in a larger circle. We give thanks knowing that we sprouted up from her, made of all of her elements, incarnated in this vessel, which we call a human body.

Just as we greet the below, we greet the above - the sun, the moon, the lights that give us life and light our way, reminding us to remember, and to be inspired to look up to the heavens which help guide us.

Then we ask to enter into the circle, we greet ourselves on this plane and the energies of this plane, and all of the beings on this plane, all of the kingdoms; the insect kingdom, the animal kingdom, the four legged, those that fly, those that crawl, those that swim, the plants and the trees, the microbes, the elements, the colors, all beings on this plane, recognizing we are just one part.

Yearning - The Taming of Connection

DIRECTION: EAST
ELEMENT : WATER

- When you look at this word what is the immediate response you have in your body?
- Where is this response held in your body?
- What are the stories you have about yearning?
- Not as familiar with the word? How about desire?

Feel into this, see where this is stored in your body and what it means to you.

Desire is a tricky one. Humans have simplified the meaning, actions and consequences of desire. Whole systems of religion have been created to address desire and not act upon it. When we look at desire as defined by the West and colonization, we have varying stances on the nature and morality of desire.

Ancient philosophers

Plato, for example, in The Republic, argued that individual desires must be deferred in the pursuit of higher ideals like justice and societal good. Aristotle explored desire as a driving force for action and distinguished between rational and irrational desires.

Early Christianity

Early Christians, often influenced by Plato, perceived dangers of worldly attachments, and often advocated for celibacy and the suppression of desires, particularly sexual desires. Sex was primarily seen as serving the purpose of procreation within marriage, with any pleasure being viewed with suspicion.

Modern Era

The Enlightenment brought a renewed emphasis on reason and individual autonomy, which some argue led to a reevaluation of desire. Desire was no longer solely condemned but also explored as a natural aspect of human experience. However, societal and cultural factors continue to shape how desire is viewed and experienced. Ongoing debates surround issues like the social construction of desire and its relationship to concepts like freedom and identity.

Buddhism

If we step outside of Western influence we have Eastern traditions, the most widely known being Buddhism, when it comes to the topic of desire. Buddhism views craving (a strong form of desire) as the root of suffering and the cycle of rebirth, advocating for its eradication to attain enlightenment or Nirvana. However, within Buddhist teachings, desire can also be directed towards skillful or wholesome ends, such as the desire to end suffering itself.

All these definitions have humans at the center of "the world", one could say, only addressing yearning as a human affair, to define as a way to separate from base desires in nature.

Now let us step into Indigenous practical wisdom, which allows us to be human and entrusts us with the ability to respond in ways wherein we stay connected to all creatures, where no beings are lesser or greater than ourselves.

We can learn from all beings how to be.

The world began with desire

There are many Indigenous stories that narrate a great energy that existed before time and space. This energy had a desire to reflect upon itself, to learn, to evolve and thus to do so divided itself to engage in reflection. This reflection took on many forms such as light, darkness, molecules, stars, cells and microorganisms that continue to change, grow and evolve, always asking the question: what is "love"?

Yearning - An alchemical reaction

The first step on the way of the feather is to accept we are creatures who yearn, who need, who desire. We are like baby birds, eyes closed, beaks open, not even able to cry yet, completely vulnerable to our needs. Nature sees this as creation itself, hungry and vulnerable and something to tend to. The West sees this as something to vilify and dominate, as seen in organized religion, and the characteristic of "the fallen human" one in which imperfection is commodified to a life path of attaining perfection through the denial of self. Yet, to yearn is to be human. When we normalize the fact we are not everything unto ourselves, then we can begin to be woven into the nest of all creation.

To change, to learn, there must be a motivation, a spark, a fire, a desire. All things begin with desire, and once we embrace this as part of our humanity instead of trying to eradicate it, then we can begin to be humans in relation to self and to the all. Even Buddhism doesn't advocate for the complete eradication of all desire. Instead, it distinguishes between healthy and unhealthy desires. Unhealthy desires, or cravings - tanha, are seen as the root cause of suffering because they lead to attachment and dissatisfaction. Healthy desires, like the desire for wisdom or compassion, can be beneficial for spiritual growth.

An alchemical reaction, refers to a transformation or process involving chemical substances, often with the goal of transmutation (changing one substance into another), achieving physical or spiritual purification. These reactions are not strictly scientific in the modern sense, but also encompass philosophical and spiritual ideas. To change one must have the ability to react and respond and go through a transformative process of physical and spiritual purification.

The key aspects of an alchemical or chemical reaction are:

Reactants: The starting materials of a chemical or alchemical reaction such as elements, ions, compounds, trauma, ideas, issues, or emotional state.

Activation energy: The energy required to initiate a reaction, the yearning to change, grow and evolve.

Transformation: This is where bonds break and new bonds are formed.

Catalyst: That which speeds up the reaction and gets consumed in the process.

Products: New substances and ways of being are formed, including a new set of possibilities/reactants for the process to begin again.

The ability to respond

Many look at responsibility as a burden, in reality, it is our ability to respond in a moment's time. When we feel the energy of yearning do we actually learn to listen to what it truly is or do we move immediately to stop feeling the sense of longing. Modern society has taught humans yearning is something to be quenched immediately. Humans then get into the habit of not having to yearn, learn or earn. Modern humans rarely have the ability to go through or hold the slow medicine of a radically transformative experience. Indigenous ways of being understand that life is a lifelong process, one could say a marathon not a sprint. We are conditioned to approach our yearnings as something that allows us the possibility of raw potential itself, not as something just "manifested" but the space and things outside our limited ability. To hold this is to let go, and invite in our yearning as an energy of activation, as a catalyst, that will burn up like a phoenix turning to ash and being reborn.

The cost of our yearning

One of the most important things about yearning and learning is understanding the cost of it. If we learn as the West would have us, it would take 7 Earths completely consumed of resources to scratch the surface of our new form of manifest destiny, the pursuit of knowledge at all costs. This is what AI is, the new excuse of colonization, whereby access to "information" and data is done at the expense of Earth, for it is deemed a greater form of knowledge.

I saw a video of a jaguar standing in front of a bulldozer protecting its home. I wept for several hours, and it still brings me to tears. There are more videos like that of Orangutans defending the forest, mother birds protecting nests in fires created by humans to clear and make space for more humans and their yearning of a promised life of convenience. The list goes on and the crimes humanity continues to perpetrate have created the horror story we are in now. Yet, we are here and must look at it, face it, realize our potential for destruction so we might realize our potential for grace. Grace amongst it all.

Indigenous people have many names for this way of life but the one I have heard around the world is, Aloha. Yes, Aloha is not a word of hello or a greeting but a state of recognition and a promise to defend the sacred within the all. Aloha- unconditional grace, mercy, compassion for the ʻāina. "Āina means land or "that which feeds", and is a central concept in Hawaiian culture, representing a reciprocal relationship between people and the land; land being the all and everything birthed from Earth Mother and Sky Father. Aloha is the grace, compassion and mercy that occurs when humans find their right place in the balance of nature. We are meant to be creatures of mercy not destruction. But when faced with separation of any kind including competition, isolation, and anything of this sort, humans are faced with their frailty. When we welcome our fragility as part of the beauty of our nature, humans are humane and seek to be connected in balance with everything and everyone. When we do not meet our frailty with grace, many times we become mercilessly, consumed by the mechanicians of "progress" which serve the few. Not many yet promise that one day you could become that few "survive".

Learning - Wisdom and Wonder

Accountability and the Formation of Habits, the Place of the Student

DIRECTION: SOUTH
ELEMENT: FIRE

Accountability: The Merriam-Webster's Dictionary defines accountability as the "obligation or willingness to accept responsibility for one's actions".

Beliefs: An acceptance that a statement is true or that something exists. Trust, faith, or confidence in someone or something. (Webster's Dictionary)

If we combine these together we have an amazing roadmap of creation.

"Your beliefs become your thoughts, your thoughts become your words, your words become your actions, your actions become your habits, your habits become your values, your values become your destiny" -Ghandi.

- **Beliefs:** What you believe forms the foundation for everything else.
- **Thoughts:** Your beliefs shape your thoughts.
- **Words:** Your thoughts are expressed through your words.
- **Actions:** Your words translate into your actions.
- **Habits:** Repeated actions become your habits.
- **Values:** Over time, these habits develop into your values.
- **Destiny:** Ultimately, your values define your destiny.

What accountability really means is being responsible for your beliefs. Understanding how they take action in your life, how they affect you, and then also how they affect others, because we all affect each other. Since we do not exist in a vacuum of thought but where the home of the mind is the body, we must be cognizant, not just of beliefs, but of biology. We have to be responsible, in understanding how we function. We have to know how our brain works, this is not knowledge or a general idea of how the human brain works, but how *your* brain works. How your body works. So many teachings out there are about mastering the mind, but so many times the biological aspect is overlooked, how our mind is wired for what we think is successful.

Learning how your vessel operates, not to conquer it but instead to be intimate with the body you have been brought to this plane with, to understand it, allows you to be connected and embodied with yourself, to show up completely and authentically as you in every situation. I'm not telling you to master your mind and your body, to negate your feelings, to do mindfulness hacks, or to hack your habits, however I do invite you to consider, are you ready for a deep and intimate relationship with yourself and to be accountable for how you operate?

Wisdom, wonder and awe - a state of being

Where is the place where wisdom and wonder meet? It is when we allow ourselves the opportunity to live a life as we pursue knowledge in a way where we're not trying to be an "expert" as society has defined. This definition of "expert" is not about "knowing" but defending, grasping, and standing apart and isolated.

Wisdom, wonder and awe are about connecting, not isolating. It is a place of being, or a feeling or a consciousness of the unknown, experiencing where your ability to respond is built on an ever changing reality, which is rooted in the reality of how this planetary system guarantees evolution through change. This can be challenging for our brains as the familiar is predictable and comfortable. The unknown is uncomfortable but that is where the alchemy of possibilities and opportunities arise.

If we look at dictionary definitions for the word wonder, as a noun, it is a feeling of surprise mingled with admiration caused by something beautiful, unexpected, unfamiliar or inexplicable as a verb. One of the definitions is desire, or to be curious to know something. The way of the feather is one of keeping a flexible mind, way and heart. This isn't about not having good boundaries. You can have good boundaries and still be flexible, continue to be in the place of the student, instead of thinking you can just sit in the north the place of the ancestors and wisdom. The wisest people I know always stay curious and flexible. They always allow themselves to understand the lesson and they come with utmost humility, to stay open knowing that the lesson can come from any being, situation, time or place, and that life is just one lesson after another, where we get to choose to grow, change and evolve.

This flexibility and curiosity takes time. It might take your whole life, yet we are so quick to master things and live a narrow life instead of allowing ourselves the curiosity and the lesson of wandering to wonder. To be responsible is then to develop the habit of meeting constant change with the wisdom of compassion, the mercy of wonder, and the joy of awe. There's no end to the wonder, the majesty; the wisdom available of the unknown is wonderful, awesome, and insightful, when met with openness, curiosity and courage.

Earning - Tending to Story

DIRECTION: WEST
ELEMENT : WIND

In conversation, it is deemed rude to talk about "earning" or in the case "worth" with reference to money. The aversion to the word reaches out beyond "society" and is used as a transactional piece, especially if using this word within a capitalistic structure, where who you are, the value of it, is tied to the amount of transaction you can afford to make.

If we start to unravel this word from capitalism, we can start letting go of preconceived notions about earning and see how it is closely related to the land and harvest.

The word "earn" has roots tracing back to Proto-Indo-European and Proto-Germanic origins. The Proto-Germanic root (aznon) connects us to the concept of "doing harvest work". If we look closely at the Old English word "earnian," meaning "to deserve, merit, or win", we see it is also connected to the concept of harvest and autumn. In Old Frisian "esna" (reward), Old Norse "önn" (work in the field), Old High German "arnon" (to reap) are all related to the Proto-Germanic root. In essence, the idea of "earning" originally encompassed the concept of hard work, especially agricultural labor, and the resulting reward or merit gained from that effort.

So earning has a time and place, it is grounded in the Earth, in harvest in autumn. In the medicine wheel for some, this is the place of the West, the place of wind and communication. It is a cycle of life in terms of age and development, as well as a yearly cycle. It is supported as a natural process.

When people come to me with many questions or wanting to learn, I tell them to plant a physical seed and tend to it as it grows. Some teachers will not accept students until they've learned to plant, grow, harvest, and process corn. Why? Indigenous teachings are closely related to land, not just in its wildness but humans in relation to its cultivation. Not the cultivation or expansion of the West which is out of balance but in relation to the sacred directions, reciprocity, gifting and permission.

I see many Western people flocking to "alternative medicine" and "teachings", yet the "new age" is not rooted in land or cultivation. Much of the new age is just Western religion repackaged with the same structures of hierarchy, and earning as a means of restoring your soul, not because it is your right and privilege as a whole being.

The Way of earning is not instagrammable

There are many ways through eons that we have shared "philosophies" of nations. Many times these are studied, argued about and unwoven in a clinical way by institutions of higher learning created by the colonizer. What happens to these ways of being in relation, to become philosophies to the outside world, is that they lose their life, they're misinterpreted, they lose their true meaning. This is beyond dilution, one might even say there is a "kill switch" or a "delete program" that is woven into words, prayers and ceremony that make them "untranslatable". Many of the "native languages" spoken today are not the original languages and words of the first people of that place; such is the case for 'Ōleo, Mexico. Most of what is shared to the general populace outside of Indigenous nations have been classified as "children's stories" because that is what white culture is has been depicted as, one in its infancy, we could even say they are stuck in their "terrible two's", defiant that their way of being is superior.

The terrible twos—characterized by defiant behavior, including saying "no," hitting, kicking, biting or ignoring rules

Environment is everything

Indigenous ways of being are not just informed but co-created with the natural environment. This is not the way of modern society, which seeks to destroy and bend nature to its will. A way that exists outside of nature can never "save", "help", "heal", nor understand ways of balance between humans as creatures and Mother Earth the way Indigenous culture does. Thus there truly is no access to these ways if one lives in the dominant world. They will always be "children stories" and so, these ways of co-creation with Mother Earth are easily forgotten or disregarded.

The poetry of Indigenous language "is"

Many find calm in the poetry of our prayers, stories and language. It is because we live this way, we walk this way, we dream this way, we play this way. It is "calming because it is connected". Our words mean what they mean, they are not romantic possibilities they "is" as some would say. Our words hold connection in a way that contains sovereignty of all beings, not dominance, that is why they feel soothing and freeing.

The Navajo/Diné traditional prayer is called "The Beauty Way" and is just one of many examples.

Here it is - Diné - The Navajo, the name for their nation—translated into English.

In beauty I walk
With beauty before me I walk
With beauty behind me I walk
With beauty above me I walk
With beauty around me I walk
It has become beauty again
It has become beauty again
It has become beauty again
It has become beauty again

Hózhóogo naasháa doo
Shitsijí' hózhóogo naasháa doo
Shikéédéé hózhóogo naasháa doo
Shideigi hózhóogo naasháa doo
T'áá altso shinaagóó hózhóogo naasháa doo
Hózhó náhásdlíí'
Hózhó náhásdlíí'
Hózhó náhásdlíí'
Hózhó náhásdlíí'

"If can, can. If no can, no can"

How do we retain the power of our words and their meaning? Practicality is a hallmark of Indigenous way and living, there is no need to use energy for superficial and superfluous things, such as "maybe". In Hawai'i there is a saying "If can, can. If no can, no can". Simply, if you can do something you should do it. If you have the ability, capacity, time, then "do it". Perfection is not expected, because we know to err is to be human. So do it and fall forward instead of never. If you can't do it, then don't, but don't spend your time justifying why. Stay empowered in creation by doing what you say. One way to do this is to tend to your story, to tend to the tree you speak about, not just take a picture and post it on Instagram. Stories do not belong to an author, they belong to people and the people must birth and tend to the stories. To tend to a story means the recognition of you as a being in community. You belong, not as an isolated character or instinct of manifestation but you are the prayer of your ancestors, human and non-human, as well as the creation of this moment in time. Yes, time as a being and cycle of creation has a consciousness that nature is keenly in tune with.

Earning - Protocol

This word has several meanings and uses based on the situation and the culture of that situation. I find the intersections of two of these meanings quite interesting.

Protocol:

(N) "A system of rules that explain the correct conduct and procedures to be followed in formal situations"

(N) "A plan for a scientific experiment or for medical treatment"

-2026 Encyclopedia Britannica

Both of these imply a series of actions or systems to be followed, to be respectful, to discover something new. If you add tradition to this there seems to be a solidification of "age old ways". This is within the framework of the West not the Indigenous. There will always be those that call themselves "fundamentalist" or those who go by "the written word" of things but Indigenous ways are not written, for they understand that life is not to be captured and contained but to ever evolve.

One of my favorite quotes from Grandfather Moonwalker was "why don't you try it, if it sticks in 100 years they will call it a tradition", and then he would laugh.

Tried and true is not the protocol we are speaking of.

We are in an interesting time where what the West would call "younger elders", are asked to step up and bring back old traditions and weave them for these times. The challenge remains that the Earth in which these traditions occurred and once were effective/ worked no longer exists. Due to human advancement of climate change and modern society, Earth's life force energy does not allow for the same conditions and support to hold this development. Instead it is harder these days to earn back the connection for Earth to support protocol but the protocols themselves will not lead to the same results because life has changed. Protocol in Indigenous ways recognizes that the "constant" of the experience is the deep reciprocal connection one must earn to be in good relation.

Earning is not done in a straight line but in a circle. Western culture is built on a philosophy or blueprint of square and line, while Indigenous cultures follow the circle as its philosophy or blueprint. Why is this important to consider? Because while you might think of them as just shapes, these are some of the basic blueprints of all creation. It is significant to note that there was one attempt that tried to mirror the old with the new and that was the story of Arthur and the knights of the round table. Using this imagery more familiar with many, we can see how and why it was created. One of the reasons was to create balance, and true humility; no one is greater or lesser than the rest. While many see this only as a political move, circled around Celtic storytelling, some say it has ties back to Charlemagne, Rome and the birth of Christian Europe and the Western Church.

Prior to Charlemagne and the fall of the Western Roman Empire, the Romans knew that all roads led to Rome, the centre of their Empire. Look at the Colosseum, which the empire built to revitalize Rome after 69 CE, a time of tumult due to the four emperors that reigned before this . The Romans used the circle for entertainment, storytelling and a way to showcase their power over those they brought home to Rome in the form of gladiators and slaves. Yet how did Rome conquer the world? With a line, with their roads which created the most direct path to "civilization". Here we start to see the use of line as a way to direct energy, give purpose and value, get from one direction to the other. It becomes a cultural sign of dominance, manifest destiny, and colonization as well as adventure, travel, and connection.

Fast forward, we see the avant-garde of the industrial area decimating circular life even more and creating the assembly line of efficiency, which humans become dependent on, and serve to tell the story of their life and value. Why? The use of an assembly line meant a division of labor, whereby unskilled workers could be trained to do one thing in repetition. The move away from craft and skilled labor, created a shift of value from bespoke goods and knowledge to mass production and speed. This creates a culture of compartmentalized relationship and knowledge where what you know, "the one thing you are trained to know" becomes your only truth. Thus creating people disconnected from the whole process, resembling human robots, who are easily manipulated. Since there is no time for connection because you are judged on "efficiency" you keep the subject in the knowledge of a simple motion, not when or how a whole piece is assembled, nor where did it come from in nature.

The necessary struggle of earning

The West sees this journey as a failure and an unnecessary use of "productivity" and time, and deems struggle as counterproductive. This is how it justifies the heralding of AI. AI is robbing us of our earning, instant gratification and access is robbing humans of the fundamental moment of the journey of a transcendental epiphany. Our journey has not become a journey but a consumption of "finished" fast made products. The struggle of the artist, writer, poet or any creative is a necessary struggle, it teaches us of our humanity and the potential of vulnerabilities. Our failures as well as successes come hand in hand. The journey of earning is the journey of accepting a fundamental aspect of humanity, we are makers of mistakes. We learn like all creatures through our mistakes, not only through our successes. We live in a colonial world that hides the mistakes and so no one knows how to achieve anything. This success is truly unachievable in this way.

Letting Go and Reciprocity

DIRECTION: North
ELEMENT: Earth

Leaving your wisdom at the door

Indigenous ways of teaching, when approached, ask you to leave your wisdom at the door. What door? This refers to the door of a lodge. What does that mean? It means you must leave your expertise, your need to know and conquer the perspective presented, the need to have answers, outside of the circle. One can not use the feedback of their desire being met in a particular way to gauge if they have learned that which is being presented. There should be no expectations and there are no certificates in these circles. To better understand the cultural challenge of stepping into these circles, let's try to clarify a few things, especially the roles in Western society tied to "knowing" or expertise.

The confusion in Western definition and role of teachers, healers and coaches.

When it comes to teachers and healers in spiritual spaces, the West have a very different expectation of experience. Also the roles many times are "interchanged" with the creation of the "coach", because many think giving advice is teaching, it is not. Yet the world is hungry to not take responsibility and accountability for their life and would find a way to blame someone else for their actions or inaction.

As we have seen, the education system around many "first and second nation" countries continues to be a place of indoctrination instead of a place of teaching critical thinking, deep relationship and accountability. What emerges from these systems are trained "accomplished" humans of which many "succeeded", not by passing grades but by copying others, to egotistically and mindlessly pass the problems onto the next generations and teachers.

In Combination with the emergence of opinions as facts, and societies and dominant cultures using their privilege to justify their expertise, we have uneducated, untrained, Western teachers, healers and coaches who are not accountable to anyone being the "guardians of what is good and bad". These days. "Healers and coaches" teach "what brings you joy" or define what is acceptable behavior as you "live your best life" free of consequences, because if you do what they say you are a good person but this is not the case.

This reality is not the reality of true healers, teachers and coaches and this reality and way is not how I was taught and trained. I have always had teachers and I have always had healers. My teachers have always had experiences of life, even if they had no PHD's or "weekend certifications" as defined by the western culture. Some have western university degrees however they all have embodiment of knowledge, wisdom, but most importantly deep relationship; something that cannot be *taught* in an education system. While the healers I worked with trained me on my natural gifts there was always a delineation of responsibility in each role and how each one was different.

Why?

Because hands heal and mouths teach. Hands cook and mouths eat. If you put your hands into someone's mouth they will bite you.

Saviorship as a wound

The idea of saviorship is wounded wisdom many can not leave behind. The need to be the expert of someone else's experience is tied closely to the fact that so many in the West have not been taught to sit with unease and discomfort or to accept the reality that this world has suffering. Why? The West is the solution to suffering, as it so has stated. In that mindset you have problem solvers with an inability to have boundaries and listen to the real needs of someone. I have found so many healers who have not learned proper boundaries and protocols who go around without asking, "healing" people, or telling them how they should live their lives to fulfill the promise of colonization. Remember colonization is a societal disease and the West does not like treating the main cause of disease only the symptoms, to keep you dependent on the system. The system needs people to believe in it so it works hard to keep them in its maze, where one does not like being uncomfortable, and not knowing makes one feel unsafe and vulnerable. It makes one feel weak. If one is vulnerable, and not knowing, then one is perceived as not being in control. If one is not in control, then people can't trust you. If people can't trust you, then they can't love you. If they can't love one, then one is not safe. This need for constant feedback of knowing is very tied to survival and this is not survival in nature but society. This is the loop that the Western system keeps you trapped in, the only circle that they want you in, keeping minds busy, bodies tense and essences fragmented, instilling constant fear, gaslighting societies, and the systems provided for you give you solutions for problems they created.

The art of the journey

Traditionally, it takes years to approach Indigenous teachers and you are supposed to be rejected by them for a period of time to see if you really are ready. Also there is the notion that all Indigenous teachers are seeking apprentices and from my experience I can tell you this is not the case. Many know they will have no "official" apprentice because the world we are living in makes it harder to find suitable students who have the temperament to walk in Indigenous ways. Many in the West want to become an apprentice immediately, or to have the experience of being a good student. Instead, in the way I have been trained and taught, the more you advance the less your teacher is present. Why? Their job is to teach you the tools, not to carry you to your destiny. It is your job to utilize the tools whether you find them "ridiculous" or "burdensome" to your Western lifestyle. The tools and practices work much like the philosophy of "chop wood and carry water". Yet many in the West see this non interference as a reflection of their personal worth and rejection.

This is true in what we teach; the West thinks if they don't understand then they haven't received anything, teaching in this way does not guarantee the teacher ensures you understand. The human teacher is just one. You must go to the other kingdoms of this planet to learn and put these practices into action to understand them. It can take a lifetime to learn and constantly unlearn what you learn along the way. Many in the West are stuck in "the need to know" which translates in needing to be seen and influenced. The issue is compounded by the myriad of modern day coaches, teachers and healers.

Gifting, reciprocity and exchange completing the circle

I was recently asked to put together a "simple how to checklist" of how to gift the Earth. While Indigenous ways believe in practical everyday applicable tools and lessons, they come with thousands of years of relationship, teaching and a way of beingness, not a checklist. The Western world is always looking for a hack and this is not the way of Indigenous life. We look for the long road, not the short one. That's why many Western teachers create books, classes, whole belief systems and techniques by borrowing from Indigenous ways. Why? They see that a little can be profited from if they promise the end of the road and the short road, not relationship.

Before we continue let us take a moment to examine what the word gifting means to you.

What is the reaction you have to the word gifting? What are the conditions? How excited or exhausted does it make you? What's the cost, principle and traditions you have around gifting and "the perfect" gift, or should we insert sacrifice here? Now you have a working definition of gifting and all that it means to you, and that is important because at all times even as the reader you are always writing alongside as you read, inserting your own story and interpretation. That's normal for a human, especially in a modern world that has taught you to do so.

When it comes to gifting, reciprocity, and exchange within the context of Indigenous ways, where all beings have value, worth, and sovereignty, the "energy exchange" is completely different; the idea of scarcity or unworthiness does not exist. Instead we believe at the end of ourselves is the beginning of another being's expression of the universe. That is why it is beyond necessary to gift, because you are not giving from what you are not, but instead who you are. May it be a song, tobacco, money, work, or anything else from your beingness as a whole contributing to the whole in it's beingness. Gifting in this way is natural and respects the you in me and the me in you.

In many traditions, because this way of being is so ingrained, the wisdom carriers do not ask for an exchange for their work because the community supports them and knows the protocol to always gift. When I say the community supports them this is when whole villages made sure to clothe, feed, and home their wisdom carriers. They all contributed and knew the value of having wisdom carriers. When this culture is confronted with the western world, the dominant culture automatically imposes its interpretation of exchange. In this case, the Western world has latched onto the idea of "not being asked to pay" in their effort to escape capitalism which has an overwhelming yoke around value and access. They use this and their ingrained programming of manifest destiny to justify not paying anything at all for an exchange. Their is no curiosity to ask about how a culture works outside of their own. Instead they are focused on the curated experience they have been told by social media they should have. Therefore they spend the money they have on more on travel not considering the cost to earth mother for their actions. The indigenous remains exotic, a place of destination, and one of exploitation.

What is understood in many balanced indigenous circles is that the gifting is just a return back to Earth. All gifts come from her, all gifts return to her. So to be a creature of Earth, created in the likeness of creation, means we share in abundance whether we deem it "good, bad or enough". Also, when a teaching is taught, or an illness remedied, it all comes from Earth. The lessons and the medicine, even the environment where it all takes place, it all holds you. So as a being of this, what I call "biosphere", gifting, reciprocity and exchange is a natural part of the circle. To not do so would be to be apart, not a part of nature.

Gifting involves relationship

The Western world has made it a high value idea to gift without being known for reasons of pride. This plays into separation, competition, worthiness etc. In the circles at the Path of IX we always teach people to formally approach all beings when entering into conscious relationships. Why? Out of respect, and to slow you down from thinking you know. We approach all beings in a formal way, from a place of our whole beingness, this means you recognize who you are and who you are not, and from there introduce yourself. As you recognize yourself, you, all of yourself, to be known by the particular being, you allow them their own free will and choice to engage, exchange, and recognize you. There is no "I am going to hug a tree without permission" in these circles. Instead you would approach the tree, introduce yourself and ask for permission and expect conditions for the exchange, which might just be a hug back for the tree itself or others. In other words gifting, reciprocity and exchange comes from asking to engage.

Giving vs Gift

Why do I keep using the words gift and gifting instead of giving? Giving is a verb, and many times you are giving something you do not have, something you consider separate from yourself. Gifting recognizes you as the gift, whole and enough, therefore gifting is an intimate act of being recognized, seen, and acknowledged. Gifting is beyond the material but can include the material as a manifestation of you and how and what you create.

How and what to gift

It can not be overstated that the how, what, when and where to gift all come from asking to engage with Earth Mother, be it a tree, teacher, bee, or other beings. There are protocols and traditions involved, depending on the peoples and the land they come from. When a representative of a people teaches gifting, it is all based on not just an oral tradition of what to do, but thousands of years of being with the land. You can never separate the Indigenous from how -they are held by the land and an equal exchange. For starters a recommendation is how can you add value to Mother Earth and not take away more than you give?

Clean : One of the things we can always do to give back is by cleaning up the impact humans have on Mother Earth. This can be small, clean up after yourself, to have a garbage bag with you to stop and pick up contaminants to Mother Earth from the roadways or trails,

Stay local: So many want to travel to distant places to "help" Earth Mother but it is your backyard that is the daily environment which supports you. By traveling to that place to see the "poverty" or "need" with your own eyes to believe it does not exist, means you're making it about you and your Western need to have. Traveling also means you are using more of Earth's resources because you find it more interesting to help something foreign, than to nurture the need that surrounds you. Support what supports you, first, everyday. Start there and if you approach and ask to engage, you will find that the smallest weed or insect will teach you more than traveling 6,000 miles to a small Indigenous place and never gifting the land you are traveling on, let alone its people.

Sing: All is vibration, and adding to that vibration through song or dance is something many beings on this planet appreciate and many have forgotten. Why do humans fill up stadiums to hear musical performances? If humans value it, so do the other kingdoms, the birds, frogs, bees and insects that you hear buzz and call about.

What tradition do you come from?

Many try to gift from outside their traditions, which makes it, one might say, more challenging because you are not gifting (that from your wholeness) you are giving. You have no long term lineage relationship to be part of the exchange, so it only goes so far. Many people do not know their lineage or heritage so it is important when you are "borrowing" from another tradition you know what the exchange must be, with that tradition and lineage, because you are asking to be represented by those that hold it.

To pray, is to accept responsibility and relationship. Gifting is the acceptance of this responsibility of being in a relationship. Being in relationship, is recognizing that all belong inside the circle of life interdependently. So the idea of a circular economy is the most natural system. Yet many in their burnout of capitalism bring their wounds of relationship to this concept and the biggest unknown wounding, is the separation from Earth. Therefore they struggle with the ideology of this system for they have not returned to a sense of deep remembering and reciprocity with all creatures on this planet.

Reciprocity

This exchange is not a competition, nor is equal exchange "equal" like down the middle. So many people give what they think another needs or wants, never actually asking. Gifting and reciprocity then becomes a proving of oneself knowing. Reciprocity is relationship and negotiation, negotiation is exchange and discourse, and our modern world loves to hide behind screens and fast checkouts instead of knowing that engagement is part of reciprocity. I read a fact that people on the internet, when checking out a new website, will not engage with it if it as some industry marketers "snap". What does that mean? A maximum 3 second upload, and 3 seconds to decide if you will engage and buy. 3 seconds. My teachers and I have gone back and forth for years over small and large topics. With my students we negotiate and negotiate exchange and reciprocity continuously. There is no quick checklist for reciprocity, nor one protocol of how to, it is about coming to the circle to sit and talk and find what works for all involved.

What am I exchanging and gifting back for writing this? Well a few things, feeding the animals on our rescue farm, who have been patient as I take time to write this, pulling weeds, watering greenhouses, lending my wife this computer since theirs is down, stirring the cacao beans that are fermenting, singing a song of gratitude, and honoring my ancestors. Gifting, reciprocity and exchange is how we live and breathe, all in *deep relationship.*

PART II

How to Gather Feathers

I wanted to take a little bit more time to invite the teachings of the feather to start to weave in their ways. There will be many opportunities however I invite you to to go out and ask the Bird Kingdom for a feather to be provided, to be shared with you and for you and in exchange to gift a song, tobacco, cornmeal or water a favorite tree or flower for these birds. When that feather comes you approach it and ask it to be with you in this circle. The way I have been taught to approach is to approach things in a very formal way. The reason is that formality makes you pause, it also adds value. Many times we disregard wisdom that is sitting right in front of us because we come from transactional exchanges, of taking and dominating everything, and we forget that a simple shift in how we approach relationship will open a door of story, of myth, where all the kingdoms, not just humans, tell their stories to teach us. So when that feather is presented, you present yourself to the feather and state your full name and that you come with great humility. You have to be specific about what you want from this feather, and that you are asking it to sit with you in this circle, and to teach you, to allow you to witness yourself.

Take some time to really tune into the feather/listen/hear the feather . If the feather does not agree then you thank it and let it go, still gifting it with song, tobacco, cornmeal, or whatever it asks of you. If it says yes, see where and how it wants to be with you and sit with you; whether it wants an altar or if it wants to reside on its own or in the comfort and support of other relationships, such as the mineral kingdom or the flower kingdom. If you do create an altar (which I highly suggest you do) make sure that you include representations of all of the elements: Water, Fire , Earth, and Wind. The Bird kingdom has so much to teach us so that it can open itself up and we can open ourselves up to a different way of learning. So with that, this is the invitation to approach. I invite you to gather your feathers and connect.

"Meaning of Feather"

As humans we love to create meaning out of everything. Many times we have a tendency to be anthropomorphic (make things human). The "meaning" we will teach here is based on our ancestors' ways of observation that are grounded and practical.

Feather Meanings

Eagle

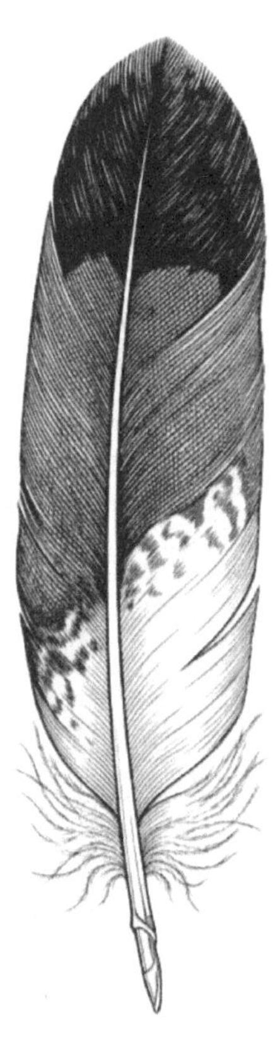

Eagle

Nesting Habit:

Require tall, mature trees, particularly coniferous and deciduous trees, for nesting and perching, often near the water. As part of the courtship process, both male and female eagles will work together to build or repair their nest.

Mating, Incubation of Eggs and Raising Young:

Eagles use "cartwheeling" (locking talons and spiraling downwards) or "death spirals" (similar to cartwheeling but with a focus on the potential for danger) as part of their courtship to assess a mate's fitness and trustworthiness.

Bald eagles are generally monogamous and will mate with the same partner for life, returning to the same nest each year.

Both the male and female eagles share the responsibility of incubating the eggs. Both parents also participate in feeding and raising the young eaglets.

Migratory Pattern: Bald eagles in particular, exhibit partial migration, with some remaining in their breeding territories year-round while others migrate south or to coastal areas in winter to find open water and food. Golden eagles, especially those in the east, are more migratory

Diet: hunt a variety of prey, including small mammals, birds, and carrion

Habitat : generally include areas near water sources like rivers, lakes, and coastlines, with mature trees for nesting and perching. Found in

Canada and Alaska, all of the contiguous United States, and northern Mexico.

The lesson: Eagle is closely related to water, tall trees, building strong bonds of family and balancing the raising of the next generation. Never taking more than it needs, it shares its hunt, and protects its nuclear family. Migratory at times it adjusts to changing circumstances and conditions. It soars heights to be able to navigate and get a clearer picture of its environment when hunting.

Therefore finding an eagle's feather is about fealty, preservation and sharing of resources. When getting bogged down with everyday needs, eagle teaches us to have a larger perspective.

Blue Jay

Blue Jay

Nesting Habit:

Nests are made of twigs and well hidden in trees and shrubs, 1–30 meters above ground. Blue jays are cosmopolitan birds that thrive in a variety of wooded habitats, especially near oak and beech trees. They are more common in smaller woodlots and forest edges than in deep forests, and have adapted to nesting in cities and towns

Mating, Incubation of Eggs and Raising Young:

Blue Jays typically form lifelong monogamous bonds and breed between March and July, building a cup-shaped nest together. The female lays a clutch of 2–7 eggs, which are then incubated by both parents for 16-18 days, with the female often doing most of the incubation and the male providing food. Parents feed and care for the nestlings for 1-2 months after they hatch, depending on their level of independence.

Migratory Pattern:

Not all migrate, only a portion of the population migrates each year, often in small, loose flocks. These migrations are diurnal (daytime) and driven by resource availability, especially during poor mast (acorn) years, though individual migration behavior varies year-to-year.

Diet:

They are omnivores, eating a variety of insects, nuts, fruits, grains and human scraps, sometimes egg and nestlings. Acorns being their favourite, they grasp them with their feet and break the shell revealing the fruit inside. They often mimic other birds including hawks to deter other birds from feeders as other birds often dominate Blue Jays. They are resourceful with their body when collecting food, using their feet, bill and holding food stores in their expandable throat pouch.

They often hide foods for a later time, which they can forget about which aids the forests to regenerate .

Habitat:
Forests, in particular forest edges and near oak trees and in wood lots. They have also adapted into suburban and urban areas, in parks and tree filled areas, in the north, east and centre of the United states and also Canada.

The Lesson:
Tight knit family systems and a variety of levels of independence from young, *if the young is disturbing and chooses to detach from the family, they are only fed if they come back to the nest, regardless of their cries.* They are intelligent and communicate with each other vocally, with an extensive vocabulary and have many different calls. Blue Jays are forward thinkers; very sharp with their intentional actions and known for their expression and use their crest as body language.

They contribute to regeneration of the forests they live in by providing an ecological service to its habitat as an unconscious decision.

Therefore, finding a Blue Jays feather is about adaptability in our surroundings and with what the wild presents to us, navigating through life's challenges, using our integrated embodiment and relationships with The All as our resources, thinking ahead whilst still engaging with traditional family value systems and our own lineage.

Hummingbird

Hummingbird

Nesting Habit:
A female hummingbird builds her tiny nest 10-40 ft from the ground and close to water, using soft fibres and feathers, animal fur, lichen moss, often on a small tree or shrub branch, somewhere hidden out of sight from predators, away from large branches where the nest will be protected from extreme weather conditions. She uses her long bill as a needle and spider silk as thread, weaving the nest together in a fine circular motion. The nests are small but because the spider silk has elastic-like qualities, they are durable. The hummingbird uses her own small frame to shape the flexible nest and her feet to compress the soft fibres to mould everything into a cup shaped nest together. The nests are tiny but pliable and expand with the baby hummingbirds. The nest is usually only used once however if the foundation is strong enough it may be used for the next.

Mating, Incubation of Eggs and Raising Young:
Females chose their mating partner according to the male's bright colours and ornamentation, including their long tail, signifying good genetics. They flaunt their beautiful and bold colours to impress the female. Female hummingbirds feed and raise their nestling on their own after incubation. It is rare that the male helps the mother as the males are polygamous. She incubates 2 eggs per brood and feeds them for 2-3 weeks until they leave the nest themselves.

Migratory Pattern:
Their migration is dependent on weather related conditions, and they opt to migrate when they see the days becoming shorter. Many hummingbirds migrate to warmer weather, basing their migration on

where there are available nectar reservoirs for them to survive. Their migration involves travelling large distances and before they migrate, they generally gain 25-40% of their body weight to support their migration because of their high energy consumption.

Anna's hummingbirds stay in their region for the winter as they are quite territorial, as do other hummingbirds from the pacific coast and California.

Diet:
Rich nectar sources with a higher sugar content, they are drawn to long red pink and other bright tubular flowers. Their long beaks are shaped to fit into a flower to drink their nectar and their diet is supplemented with insects and spiders.

Hummingbirds metabolise very quickly as they're constantly using so much energy. Their heart rate beats over 1000 times per minute, they flap their wings over 80 times per second and their oxygen consumption is so high resulting in needing constant feeds during the day. If there is not enough food supply, they risk starvation. At night they enter a state of rest called torpor which is a nightly hibernation for them, especially in the winter, to preserve their energy stores.

Habitat:
Requires deciduous and cloud forests, rain forests, woodlands, grasslands, orchards, gardens and many urban and suburban landscapes. Crucially, somewhere where there is an abundance of flower variety, or nectar feeders and safe shelter for them to rest safely at night. They are found in the Americas and their habitat is so diverse because there are hundreds of species of hummingbirds.

The Lesson:
Their vibrant feathers are not a pigmented colour but a prism-like cell

in their feather structure which changes when it reacts to light and differs within each observer and the angle viewed.

They are closely related to flowers, water, heights and peculiar movement. They have co-evolved with nature as they contribute to the pollination by drinking flower nectar for food survival. They migrate great distances and at a fast pace, in ways a bird doesn't usually move; Their unique shoulder joints attached to their wings and rotates 180 degrees in a figure 8 motion and is the only species of bird that does this. They hover up, down and in one place and can also fly backwards. They preserve energy during the evening and provide protection for their young in their intricately constructed nests until they're fully equipped.

Therefore, finding a Hummingbirds feather is about attention to details, moving with integrity yet resilience and adaptability because of their small bodies, discernment and perseverance with the preservation of energy and reminding us with their colours that things may not always be as they seem and to stay present.

Cardinal

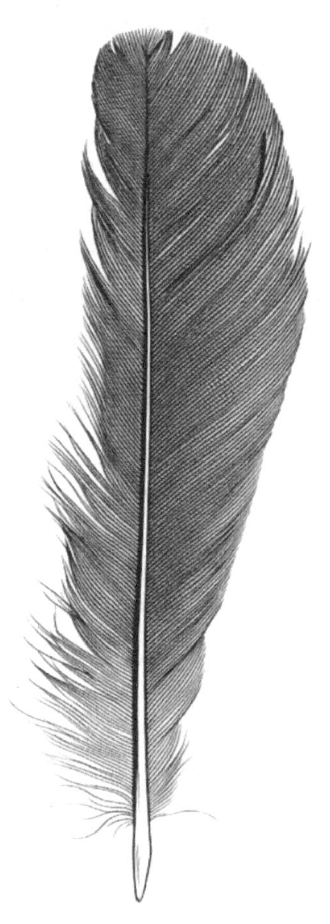

Cardinal

Nesting Habit:
Nests made in forks of branches of the trees, 3-10 feet off the ground, are low and well hidden in dense foliage; shrubs, thick tangled vines and shrubs, where there is protection and accessibility.

The female cardinal will pick the nesting spot with the male accompanying her on this quest, she predominately builds the nest. The male assists by gathering materials and feeding during nidification to show his ability to take care of their brood, providing food and security for the fledglings. Her colour is not as bright as the male cardinal; this helps her to blend in during incubation and whilst caring for her brood as protection against predators. She creates a cupped nest created from stems, grass, bark, and twigs that are broken by the female cardinal to mould into shape for the nest.

Mating, Incubation of Eggs and Raising Young:

Serial monogamy for the season and sometimes for life, males displaying courtship to the female and defending their mating partners, offering them food as gifts. Their breeding begins in march until September, averaging 2 - 3 broods per year with 1-5 eggs. Incubation occurs by the female and the eggs take 10-13 days to hatch. Males and females both gather food for their fledglings as they're born altricial, enough food is critical for their survival. They both share the responsibility of raising the young Cardinals and teaching them about foraging possible threats.

Migratory Pattern:

They do not migrate, they are territorial. They remain in their breeding grounds in large flocks of cardinals and other species, foraging with them in low branches or on the ground.

Diet:

Omnivore, eating fruits, seeds, grains however also eating insects.

Habitat:

Found in North America, Bermuda and the Hawaiian Islands. They roost in wetlands, woodland edges, shrublands, very dense trees or shrubs by streams, gardens, saplings, dense foliage, and suburban and urban areas in backyards and birdfeeders with sunflower seeds. 1-15ft off the ground. High perches for singing.

The male cardinals are territorial during breeding season, if they see their own reflection they try to fight it, however they are social birds in the non-breeding season.

The Lesson:

Cardinals sing a variety of different melodies, they are known as songbirds. Male Northern Cardinals are known for their bright red plumage, that cannot be missed, they confidently protect their territory, and nurture their mate, especially during mating season when they are vulnerable to predators such as snakes, squirrels and other birds. They spend time in trees and on the ground foraging.

Therefore, finding a Cardinal feather is about encouragement to sing and express our own melody through all seasons whilst being bold, also reminding us to energetically shield ourselves and our environments, understand and nurture our surroundings.

Dove

Dove

Nesting Habit:

Requires dense foliage on the branch of trees or in a vine or large shrubs. Dove's nests are made from twigs, pine needles, stems, mostly and grass in a bowl shape, generally flimsy. The male helps to collect the materials, and the female builds the nest. The nests location is established by the male suggesting a site with his nest soliciting call; however ultimately, the female dove chooses the site. Most species will use a nesting box and are not afraid of humans.

Mating, Incubation of Eggs and Raising Young:

Most species are monogamous, pairing for life. 1-3 eggs are laid 8-12 days after mating and hatch after 14- 18 days. Doves have 2 – 3 broods per year and 6 in warmer climates. Young doves will stay by the nest for the first week or 2 after hatching and rely on their parents for feeding.

Migratory Pattern:

Depending on the species of doves, some do migrate, they are partial migrants. Doves from South America do not migrate however those from North America migrate to the south. They migrate seeking seasonal food resources and warmer climates. Some species of Doves migrate shorter distances than others and the doves that do not migrate seek warmth and shelter in buildings.

Diet:

Seeds, grains and fruits. Doves forage on the ground and in the open on roadsides, in backyards, in fields and grasslands. A portion of dove species eat cereals, legumes, weeds, fruit and can supplement with small invertebrates.

Habitat:

They thrive in a large variety of environments, deciduous forests, urban and suburban settings, swamp forests, agriculture settings, deserts, grassy plains in tropical and subtropical regions. Doves can be found all around the world, except Antarctica and they thrive on sea level and some species up to 16,000 feet.

The Lesson:

Doves have learnt to live and thrive in all different environments; however, they are particularly skilled in finding their way back home. Doves have been used as messengers for thousands of years because of this impeccable skill, using the Earth's magnetic field, internal mapping and their own solar compass. They have great strength and speed, endurance, adaptability and agility

Therefore, finding a Doves feather is a reminder that the body remembers, and trust that you will always find your way back home *to yourself.* It reminds us that our ancestors have all endured so much and that we are adaptable to a diverse array of environments, however our bodies will always remember what it feels like to be home

Woodpecker

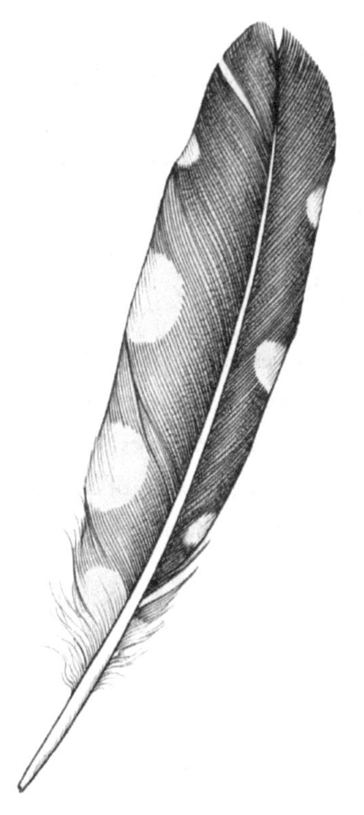

Woodpecker

Nesting Habit:
Cavities in trees that a woodpecker excavates is where woodpeckers nest. Dead trees, often with rot disease, make the tree's centre softer, which makes the excavation process of the cavity easier on the woodpecker. During the excavation process bark that falls into the cavity and is used as a bed for the eggs. There is no typical other nesting material used, and a number of species return to the same cavity for nesting.

Gila woodpeckers chisel holes in the saguaro cactus well in advance before mating season so the cavity can cure in preparation for the incubation period. Their homes are typically in treeless deserts. The cactus dries out around the cavity and then it is finally ready for use.

Of over 240 species of woodpeckers, the ground woodpecker and the Campo Flicker dig their nest cavities in the ground.

Woodpecker's homes are used by secondary cavity nesters including squirrels, bluebirds, swallows and some owls and duck species and others as they cannot excavate their own cavity.

Mating, Incubation of Eggs and Raising Young:
Most species are monogamous; some find a mate for 1 season and then they part. The mating begins with male courtship of drumming with his bill. Varying amongst the woodpecker species, they lay between 3-7 eggs. Males incubating eggs during the night and alternating with the female for 10-14 days and both helping to raise the young. They are born altricial and are in the nestling period for 18-35 days. The female may hatch more or less eggs depending on food availability.

Acorn woodpeckers and red-cocked woodpeckers have a more complex social system compared to others. Their young stay with them for several years (mostly from the sons) and help to raise the newer fledglings; often more than 1 female is laying eggs.

Migratory Pattern:
Not all woodpeckers migrate, roughly a third of the species migrate by virtue of their food resources and are temperate zone species, seeking warmer climates, the rest are resident. The red headed woodpecker is migratory and may be found in a location one year but not the next.

Diet:
Their long bills (some Woodpeckers with extremely long barbed shaped tongues) allow them to probe grubs and insects from trees. They are omnivores, eating a combination of insects, seeds, nuts, spiders, acorns and other nuts, fruit, and small birds. A portion of woodpeckers species drink nectar and sap from certain trees at specified times. Acorn woodpeckers store acorns around in tree cavities and various locations such as buildings, so they have food throughout all the seasons. Woodpecker's species hearing is so good that they can hear insects crawling and chewing in trees.

Habitat:
Requires open woodlands and deciduous woodlands, dense forests, deserts, dead trees. Woodpeckers are found everywhere in the world except for Australia and New Guinea. They occur most in South America and southeast Asia. They roost in cavities, which are often different to the ones they breed in.

They spend so much time 'pecking' into trees, their brains are protected by special mechanisms in their body. Woodpeckers use their bills to drum as a form of communication. Over time the woodpecker biology has advanced; in present times, living most of their life in trees, woodpeckers, besides 2 species, have 4 toes (American three-toes and the black-backer have 3), 2 pointing forward and 2 pointing backwards (zygodactylism).

The Lesson:
The stiff tail of a woodpecker is used as a third leg, to give them stability whilst climbing up the tree or hopping from tree to tree or branch. Woodpeckers zygodactylism helps woodpeckers with stability when pecking wood, climbing trees, grasping, giving them more support for their journeys above and below. Ecosystems forest engineers, creating cavities for other animals that require cavities but cannot excavate them and have created body mechanisms within themselves for protection for their excavations.

Therefore, the feather of a Woodpecker is about living in balance with the environment, following the beat of your own drum, no matter how loud it is. Holding yourself as your own pillar, trusting your own stability, and that the ripple effect of your own actions is larger than you think.

Magpie

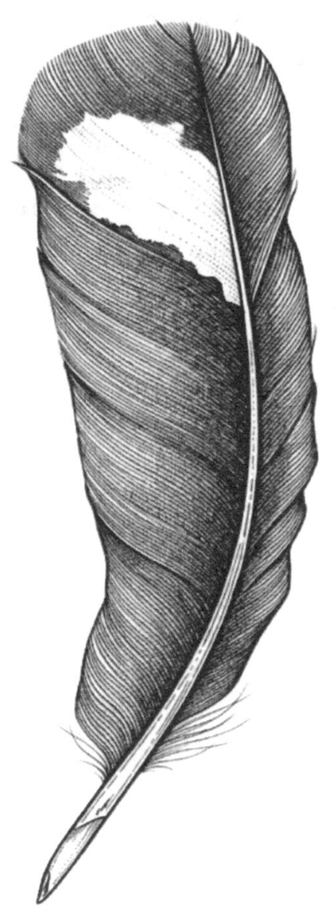

Magpie

Nesting Habit:

In tall trees 10-15m above the ground on a branch or on the fork of a tree, some species in dense trees and thorny bushes. Female magpies are in charge of building a large bulky dome shaped nest, with the male and female gathering supplies.

If magpies have had a successful nesting habitat raising offspring in the past, they will often return to the same spot. This is dependent on water and food supplies.

Mating, Incubation of Eggs and Raising young:

Magpies are monogamous and usually have 1 mate for life and typically 1 brood per season. If the brood is not successful or if the season stays warm enough, they may try for another. Australian Magpies lay between 1-5 eggs, Eurasian magpies clutch size is 5-7 eggs, Black billed magpies clutch size is 1-9. Each species incubates for 3 weeks. The male feeds her after she hatches the eggs and defends the territory and their offspring from predators by swooping anyone or anything that they perceive as a threat around breeding times.

The hatchlings are born with their eyes closed and they're completely dependent on their parents but by the 4th week they can leave the nest and explore their surroundings. The fledglings stay with their parents for 6-8 months before becoming fully independent.

Migratory Pattern:

Magpies typically do not migrate. They are territorial and are social birds that enjoy living in groups with their families called tidings. They stick together and safeguard one another from dangers through their varied and complex calls. They also mimic other birds and human voices.

Diet:

They will feed on whatever is available seasonally, worms, lizards, fruit and grains, grasshoppers and beetles. They are omnivores and scavengers of food scraps. They forage on the ground and steal meat from other animals. A magpie's hearing is impeccable, they are able to hear their prey in the ground and use their long beak to retrieve it.

Habitat:

Urban and suburban, wetlands, grasslands, woodland, hills and hillside, farmland, heathland, parks and playing fields, anywhere where there are trees and open lands. They have adapted to cosmopolitan life.

The Lesson:

Relating closely to trees and their own ground. They are incredibly adaptable and smart birds, methodical thinkers in their behaviours of breeding, protecting their families, and defending their territories. They reflect to us similarities in human relationships and social structures.

Therefore finding the feather of a magpie is about adaptability and duality with their black and white feathers. Magpie feathers are about noticing our surroundings and their polarities. Acknowledging them not as weaknesses, villainizing them or idealising, just witnessing yourself in the moment as a part of the moment, to alchemise, to not suppress or to subdue, but to be more harmonious.

Cockatiel

Cockatiel

Nesting Habit:
They are secondary cavity nesters and nest in large tree hollows, favouring Dead eucalyptus trees, about 2m above the ground and close to water and food supplies.

Mating, Incubation of Eggs and Raising Young:
They are monogamous and form a bond with 1 mate early in life. They stay together throughout the year as an expression of their loyalty and share bonds for more than reproductive purposes. They display courtship to one another, a male with his singing and the female with her erect tail. Their mating is triggered from large rain falls as this ensures there's resources available for them. Their breeding season is from early spring to late summer.

Both cockatiel parents incubate the eggs, males sitting diurnally and the females at night and both parents raise the chick. 4-7 eggs are hatched and incubated for 17-23 days. They will remain in the nest for 4-5 weeks.

Migratory Pattern:
Cockatiels from Australia's north and wetter climates are more nomadic; they will move based on feeding availability, whereas birds from southern Australia are more migratory. They are not territorial birds, they will relocate to wherever there are available resources.

Diet:
They are granivores. They forage on the ground and eat cultivated crops, seeds, and grasses.

Habitat:
This member of the cockatoo family is endemic to outback regions of Australia, less common in Tasmania, preferring wetlands, bushlands,

grasslands, shrublands and scrublands, acacia shrubs bordering waterholes in dryer arid or semi-arid planes, however always near bodies of water.

The Lesson:
They have complex vocalizations when communicating with each other and are known for their forms of self-expression using their body language using their crests. They do not have attachment to their surroundings, instead evolving with their environment, as secondary cavity nesters and navigating through challenges of the wild. Cockatiel's strong social bonds and communication helps them to protect themselves and their flocks by collaborating and defending each other from other predators and other challenges.

Therefore, finding a feather of a cockatiel signifies drawing on available resources that we have without attachment, caring and being in reciprocal relationships with your loved ones, fostering collaboration, and expressing your true self, openly, vulnerably and fearlessly.

Sparrow

Sparrow

Nesting Habit:
Nests are formed in protected areas, buildings, tree cavities, nest boxes, bushes, under bridges, in vines and in sufficient previously existing nests. Their nest is built by both male and female, made of wool, feathers, grass.

Mating, Incubation of Eggs and Raising Young:
Most Sparrow species form permanent bonds with another making them monogamous with the same sparrow for life, typically in the same nesting space. Their breeding season is contingent on their food provisions.

Varying amongst the sparrow species, they lay between 1-8 eggs. The eggs hatch after 10-14 days and the nesting period most common of sparrows is 14 days, fledging the nest soon after. Some may have 2-3 clutches per season.

Migratory Pattern:
A portion of Sparrow species migrate when the temperature drops seeking warmer weather and in search for food sources. The American sparrow migrates south. Other species retreat to shelter in buildings and cavities in trees. House sparrows are sedentary birds and do not migrate. Sparrows migrated with people and that is how they have made their way around the world, there are more sparrows on Earth than there are people.

Diet:
Sparrows are omnivorous birds, their diet consists of grains, seeds and berries. They also consume fruit, spiders, insects, snails and food scraps from humans. They forage on the ground.

Habitat:
Found in all continents except Antarctica. They have adjusted to suburban areas and cities, living around humans, although their natural habitat is fields, farmlands, grasslands, countryside woodlands, scrublands, and deserts.

They are social birds, often found singing in groups and colonies, except the great sparrow which prefers its own family bond. They forage in large groups, during mating season the flock becomes specified to its own type. They make indentations in the ground and are known for dust bathing.

The Lesson:
There are more sparrows in the world than people. The habitats, breeding conditions and migration of these birds are so vast that their connections to humans is very comparable as they have lived besides humans for so long including migrating with them, located in all but 1 continent.

Therefore, finding a feather from a Sparrow is about acknowledging that you are a human and having a human experience. Sparrows have adapted to our ways of being however have never forgotten the connection to the Earth or amongst other sparrows, reminding us to remember and acknowledge our own human relations and to let Mother Earth feel your presence too.

Guacamaya (Macaw)

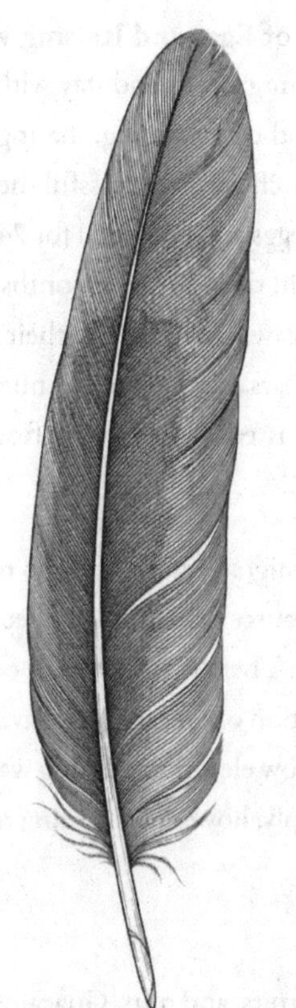

Guacamaya (Macaw)

Nesting Habit:

Guacamaya nest in nots or crevices in tall trees on higher elevations, some species on rocky cliffs for protection and a portion dig out riverbanks. They are extremely territorial regarding nest defence, often resulting in beak and claw fights. Both adults will stand in the nest cavity and defend it by screeching loudly and in a few instances, breaking another macaw's eggs to claim the cavity.

Mating, Incubation of Eggs and Raising young:

They are typically monogamous and stay with their partner for life. They look after each other, grooming, sharing food and caring for the young. 1-4 eggs hatch and if successful they won't reproduce for 2 years after. The eggs are incubated for 24-28 days and young Guacamayas will stay in the nest for 3 months, they do not leave their parents for a year. Macaws breed later in their lives, reaching sexual maturity from 2- 10 years of age which is much later in life compared to the other birds discussed. They can live from 35 up to 80 years.

Migratory Pattern:

Not all Guacamaya's migrate, and if they do move it is within the proximity, seeking resource availability, or because they are too old or too young to breed. There is an elevation component in their migration, with a portion of Guacamaya travelling from a western high point to eastern low elevation, seeking warmer climates, available habitat, and food supply, however returning to the high elevation point.

Diet:

Seeds, leaves, insects, fruits, and nuts. Guacamaya's strong beak is used to crack open hard-shelled nuts and seeds and remove the kernel with their muscular tongues. They consume clay from riverbanks commonly found in rainforests, as a rich source of minerals and to neutralize the toxins they have absorbed from their plant consumption; they are immune to poisonous fruits they consume. Their bright feather colour pigments come from their diverse and bright diet allowing them to camouflage, with similar coloured fruit, from predators in their habitat.

Habitat:

Guacamaya's are found in tropical North, Central and South America, typically in rain forests, tropical jungles, savannas and swamps, some of the species are found in arid spaces. Guacamaya's are social and intelligent, bonding in large flocks which can be over 40 and in pairs. Their beaks serve as a third leg whilst climbing up and down trees. Their calls are loud to claim their territory and to communicate with their flock and partners.

The Lesson:

Related to heights, heat, clay, tall trees and water and creating strong bonds with their mates. They are associated with the rainforest and moving for food supplies and better living environments, living high above the Earth and below, working with their environment. They are social and curious beings

Therefore, finding a Guacamaya feather is about remembering to pause and to nourish the relationships you hold with all of the kingdoms and all of the elements, and their intelligence and understanding that you encompass. They remind us to be social and nourishing and as curious as all of the colours combined about ourselves without neglect and the reminder to always lean into your own potentiality.

Pelican

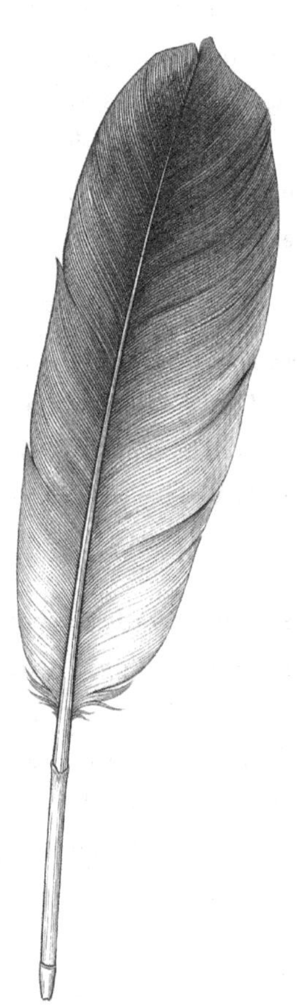

Pelican

Nesting Habit:
Creches are often nesting in larger breeding colonies, on islands or secluded seashores. 4 of 8 pelican species can nest in trees but most create scrapes on the ground lined with feathers, leaves, twigs, seaweed. In some pelican species, males display courtship by developing different colours on their pouches and throat.

Mating, Incubation of Eggs and Raising young:
Pelicans are monogamous for 1 season, after rainfall indicating ample fish for food. Breeding seasons vary geographically typically after winter, with some breeding once per season and other Pelicans at any time if food and water availability permits. 1-4 eggs laid 2-3 days apart. Their incubation period is 29-35, with both pelicans standing on their eggs to incubate them with their webbed-like feet. Australian pelican nesting period is up to 35 days, Young Brown and American white pelicans will stay in the nest anywhere between 63-84 days, born altricial - they are very dependent on their parents for resources. Young chicks will often be vocal before leaving the nest, hissing, and gaping their bills; however as they grow, they only become vocal in their breeding colony.

Migratory Pattern:
Most species are migratory before the colder months and if not migratory, they are travelling long distances in search for food. Pelicans are driven by the weather and food availability. They migrate in a V formation in their fleet which helps with their energy consumption, flying at the back takes less energy thus alternating roles in their migration.

Diet:
Primarily eating fish that surface at the water, which are easily scooped up with their massive pouched bills. American pelicans are known for their dive underwater to catch fish; this can start from 20m above the water when they spot their prey. The other species dip for their prey. American White Pelicans and Australian Pelicans work together to catch prey, synchronising their bill dipping into the water aiming at schools of fish. Pelicans also eat salamanders, other birds, crabs, and turtles.

Habitat:
Pelicans spend time in squadrons, always near bodies of fresh and salt water, mud flaps, swamps, seashores, lakes, ponds, riverbanks, estuaries, anywhere there is a fish supply for them. Pelican communication is visual rather than vocal; they are silent communicating mostly with their wings and bills. They are not found in Antarctica, preferring warmer climates, however pelicans can be found in every other continent in the world.

The Lesson:
Thriving in a range of habitats and closely related to water, the ground, warmer climates and air. Pelican species exhibit masterful flying capabilities soaring long distances without flapping, however consciously choosing to take food and rest breaks, regardless of their great flying potentiality, flying with ease sharing the load of the long flights amongst their flock. They are good swimmers not walkers and their sensory perception is heightened by its bill, adapting and eating even in murky waters.

Therefore, finding a pelican feather represents a reminder to honour our ancestors as the elements. They represent having no fear when diving into the depths of ourselves, into our own murky waters, not being afraid to soar, however remembering as human beings that we do require nurturing simultaneously. They remind us to have courage and to have humility to ask your community for support.

ʻIʻiwi (scarlet honey creeper)

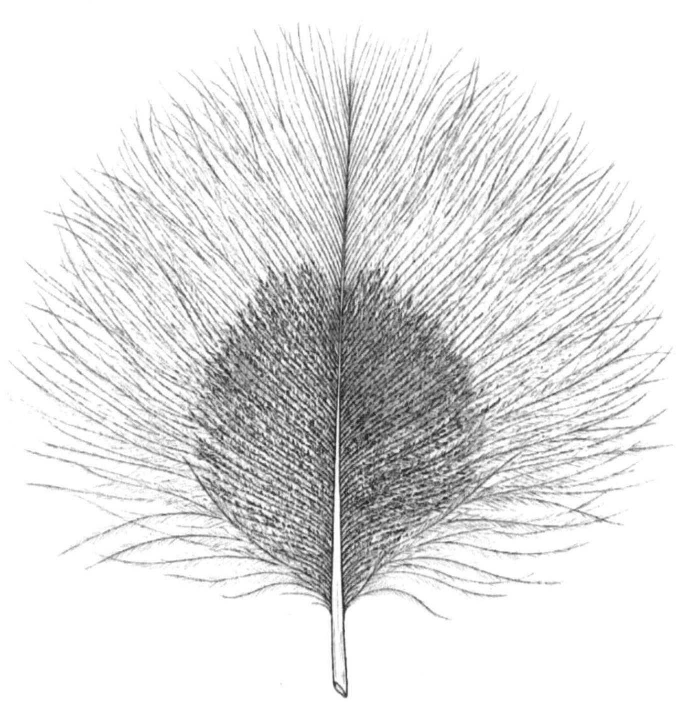

'I'iwi (scarlet honey creeper)

Nesting Habit:
Male and female 'I'iwi's build a cup shaped nest using bark fragments, feathers, petals, twigs, ferns, and lichens high up in the top, the crown of the tree, preferring an ōhia tree. Defending their breeding territory and sometimes the nectar stores.

Mating, Incubation of Eggs and Raising young:
Acts of courtship are displayed between 'I'iwi's and they are monogamous birds for the season, both feeding the young. Breeding season is any time for 'I'iwis, however peak breeding is between February to June. The female incubates 1-3 eggs for 14 days. The female 'I'iwi also looks after the young for 21-22 days during the nestling period, whilst the male feeds from the nest. The young are dependent on their parents for up to 4 months.

Migratory Pattern:
'I'iwi's follow the abundance of bloom resources, flowers. After breeding, 'I'iwi move downslope to elevations of 1200m, Their movements are driven to seek nectar reservoirs and eventually moving back up slope up to 2800m.

When 'I'iwis get closer to the grounds of wet forests, they are more prone to exposure to mosquito breeding territories, and they risk contracting avian malaria. 'I'iwi's are not immune to avian malaria and if bitten by an insect with this disease will most likely die. This is one of the factors lowering the mortality rate of this bird, others inclusive of this are climate change, humans and feral mammals all contributing to the decline of forest regeneration where their risk of contracting avian malaria increases.

Diet:

Their downward curving beak allows them to pierce tubular flowers and sip nectar from native flowers: lobeloid plants, flowering ōhia and māmane flowers, and non-native flowers. They also eat moths, spiders, and other insects.

Habitat:

Requiring wet montane and wet mesic forests, 'I'iwis are native to Hawai'i, Maui, Kauai, less in O'ahu and Moloka'i. They are found from sea level to the highest altitude forests on the islands, living closely to an abundance of nectar, and in support of their diet. They play an important role in preservation of the native landscapes of Hawaiian Islands being 'ōhio pollinators.

The Lesson:

'I'iwi are closely related to water, forests, and flowers, living and nesting in high elevations but also moving to low elevations and being strong flyers. They move with the availability of resources but, also very susceptible to disease. They understand being up above and below and adapting to the climates.

Therefore, finding a 'I'iwi feather is about the abundance of our own trees in our own forest. To learn to be comfortable with being uncomfortable living in our own terrains and to adjust to the different circumstances around us. Allowing yourself to be flexible and resilient to change. When it is time to move on, you listen to the hunger from within and allow it to move you to create space for yourself to grow.

Raven

Raven

Nesting Habit:

Requiring knots or crevices high in large trees, On cliffs edges, cliffs under a rock overhanging, on building structures like bridges and billboards, and powerlines. Raven's nests are made from sticks, moss, twigs, small branches, lined with wool, feathers, bark, grass, and fur. Nests are woven by the female into an uneven cup shape, with the male assisting in gathering materials.

Mating, Incubation of Eggs and Raising young:

Males displaying courtship to their mate with their acrobatic aerial dances, supported by their extra feathers, they usually pair up and mate for life. Sexual maturity is at around 3 years of age.

The female incubates 3-7 eggs for 20-25 days, both parents feeding and caring for the young for the nestling period of 28-50 days, having 1 brood per year. Ravens defend their territories and their resources during the breeding season from other ravens and predators.

Migratory Pattern :

Most ravens are non-migratory birds, they are primary residences, a small portion may wander in Winter and Fall

Diet:

Ravens are omnivores, eating almost anything; plant matter, eggs, insects and invertebrates, carrion consisting of small mammals and birds. Consuming carrion plays a large role in our ecosystem, assisting to prevent the spread of diseases. Ravens are known for collaborating with other ravens to hunt for prey and storing cache for later consumption.

Habitat :

Thriving in a vast array of habitats, except rainforests, they prefer open landscapes but can be found in from tundra to hot deserts; scrubby woodlands, coniferous and deciduous forests, forest lands, grasslands, deserts, mountainous regions, agricultural fields, seaside rocky cliffs, coastal, woodlands, icy floes, and urban areas. Ravens are found in Africa, south Asia, Australia and North and central America and Northern Europe.

Younger ravens travel together in their flock (conspiracy) for winter for warmth before pairing and the conspiracy of ravens often roost together in communal spaces, feeding together. They are social birds when it isn't breeding season, with vocal complexity in their sounds and an innate ability in imitating other animals and humans and remembering their faces.

The Lesson:

Ravens are closely related to being high in trees and low on the ground foraging and catching prey. Known for their aerobic dances through life, being adaptable and intelligent, having innovative solutions for complex problem solving, being one of the smartest animals on this planet and having a complex vocal system.

Therefore, finding a Raven feather is about adaptability, and remaining grounded whilst using your skills to uplift your community, soaring high with perspective and coming back to your body with solutions.

Feathering Your Nest

The gathering of feathers like any object is not solely about the object itself apart from everything. A feather might have a lesson but it is in weaving it "into a nest" or altar that you start to create, what we call in our circle, a biosphere. This is where life happens, interconnected in deep relationship.

If you enjoyed the process of finding your feather, continue learning from our ancestors, the birds, on how they build their nests. As you watch, observe and learn from the birds, one can witness how everything is in place. All woven perfectly together. Birds do this better than humans, they innately know how to weave a life connected to nature, from nature, and within the rules of nature. Make sure to feed your bird ancestors; feeding the ancestors is a crucial way to begin connecting back to all that is and has been.

If you don't know how to feed your ancestors come join us over at our print Anthology Cooking with the Ancestors where we Come to the Table with stories, recipes and even cook together online!

For those of you who observed birds that migrate, what a gift and lesson. How beautifully they depict the way to walk the circle. Join us as we walk the circle migrating between the east, south, west, and north in our online 18 month Slow Medicine circle.

There are many ways to feather your nest; weaving the land, the stories of your ancestors, and more as you continue to acclimate yourself to these ways of slow medicine.

Slow Medicine

When times become chaotic, people turn to baking, crafting, gardening, weaving, building, doing these fundamental things with our hands that drop us out of our heads, out of a sense of no-control, and that anchor us into reality that we can touch, feel, understand, and connect to.

These practices connect us to our ancestors, to the ancestors of all humanity, who at one time (or still currently) lived this way, tied to our environments, our pace controlled by the turning of seasons, our resources what was around us. When cultures become disconnected from cycles, we lose track of what real value is, because we confuse money with value. Money is not value. What is the value of a small snake, that we carve with our hands, using simple tools, sitting in a circle with companions, listening to wisdom stories, our bodies learning the feeling of not having to perform anything in order to belong?

Is it less than the value of an app that makes someone millions of dollars? Or is it perhaps more? Working with our hands can help show us the way home. Our ancestors' hands can guide our hands, as we make sacred tools. As we sit with rocks, and earth, and water, and fire, and air. As we sit with grains, seeds, wood, feathers, string, and stone. We will listen , we will build, we will walk, we will learn .

What is the value of traveling through the four directions together, learning from the seasons, and weaving these lessons into the things we make? These are times for slow medicine. We need each other, we need to anchor into something real. How can your ancestors' hands guide you, when they cannot catch you, even for a moment?

Your attention is the commodity that the modern world is most hungry for.

And the busier your attention is, the faster you will forget. You will be too busy to question the lies of modernity: That we will only thrive if we give up our connection to Earth and to each other. You can forget your incredible potential for *- luminosity.* As humans, we easily forget. But our ancestors knew this. Our ancestors knew that living in rhythm with nature reminds us that we do not have to spend our whole lives searching in order to belong.They knew that our search for belonging ends when we reconnect to the truth: that you belong to the Earth (even if you're a starseed).

Our lineages carry ritual and protocol to stay in connection. By slowing down together in circle, we make space for our ancestors' hands to guide us home to these practices. We can ground this ancestral knowledge with the physical making of sacred tools, which represent and hold all the blueprints of creation. An entire universe, contained in one little piece of creation. The cycle of the circle is the cycle of life.We are not in a competition or a race when we work with slow medicine

. We recognize each other as complete, unique, interdependent, and necessary within the whole.

It is by embracing the natural rhythms of creation, the blueprints of life that we are a part of and from,

That you will FINALLY experience being enough.

You are enough.

THANK

Did you know preceded of Way of the Feather go to animal rescue !!

NEW BOOKS !!

CHECK THEM OUT! *We hand-picked them for you!*

IK': 3 BREATHS

FOR CHILDREN AND ADULTS

Celebrating indigenous artists.

What if three simple breaths could bring us back to ourselves, to each other, and to the Earth?

This is the invitation of Ik: 3 Breaths - a sacred children's book gifted through a dream, brought to life with beautiful illustrations, and rooted in ancestral teachings. It is more than a book; it is a path of remembrance.

A 30 DAY JOURNEY OF THE HAWAIIAN MOON PHASES

By Vesna Vavladellis & One Who Catches Lightning and Keeper of the Thunderstone

Join us as we pray, plant, and drink cacao for 30 days of transformational change.

LINK TO BIG LITTEL LIFE PUBLISHING >>>

ONLINE CLASSES

Join us in cultural exchanges with our partners

We work with elders to connect you back to the soil. These self lead THINKIFIC Classes are great ways to explore decolonization and enter into a realm where all is connected.

SCAN QR CODES TO DISCOVER MORE!

ALL MONEY FROM THESE CLASSES GO TO INDIGENOUS ELDERS, LAND RESTORATION, AND RESCUE ANIMALS

CULTURAL EXCHANGE

THE WAY OF THE FEATHER

AN INVITATION TO "LEAVE YOUR WISDOM AT THE DOOR"

Hawaiian Cacao

HEARTH EARTH DRUM

www.ingramcontent.com/pod-product-compliance
Lightning Source LLC
LaVergne TN
LVHW040221110826
845146LV00005B/1370

* 9 7 9 8 9 9 5 4 3 6 8 0 5 *